make

precut quilts

10 Dazzling Projects to Sew

C&T PUBLISHING

Text, photography, and artwork copyright © 2016 by C&T Publishing, Inc.

Publisher: Amy Marson

Creative Director: Gailen Runge

Project Editor: Alice Mace Nakanishi

Compiler: Lindsay Conner

Cover/Book Designer: April Mostek

Page Layout Artist: Casey Dukes

Production Coordinator: Zinnia Heinzmann

Photography by Diane Pedersen, Christina Carty-Francis, and Nissa Brehmer, of C&T Publishing, unless otherwise noted

For further information and similar projects, see the book listed after each artist's bio.

Published by C&T Publishing, Inc., P.O. Box 1456, Lafayette, CA 94549

Attention Teachers: C&T Publishing, Inc., encourages you to use this book as a text for teaching. Contact us at 800-284-1114 or ctpub.com for lesson plans and information about the C&T Creative Troupe.

Printed in China

10 9 8 7 6 5 4 3 2 1

Contents

2½″ STRIPS AND 5″ SQUARES

10″ SQUARES

Precuts	Also called
2½″-wide strips	Jelly rolls, Roll-Ups
5″ × 5″ squares	Charm squares, charm packs
10″ × 10″ squares	Layer Cakes

Summer Sorbet

Rachel Griffith

Bright stars twinkle among colorful nine-patch squares in this fun summery quilt that combines prints and solids in an easy-to-make design.

Made by Rachel Griffith; quilted by Darla Padilla

RACHEL GRIFFITH is a self-taught quilter who has become a quilt teacher, designer, blogger, book author, magazine contributor, and has her own pattern line as Rachel Griffith Designs. She lives near Cleveland, Ohio.

WEBSITE: psiquilt.com

This project originally appeared in *Fresh Fabric Treats* by Moda Bake Shop designers, available from Stash Books.

Materials and Cutting

CHARM PACKS:

    2 prints (I used Fandango.)

    3 neutral solids (I used Bella Oatmeal.)

    3 pastel solids (I used Bella Warm Pastels.)

AQUA FABRIC: ½ yard for inner border

    Cut 8 strips 1½″ × 45″.

CORAL FABRIC: 1½ yards for outer border

    Cut 8 strips 5½″ × 45″.

BINDING FABRIC: ¾ yard

    Cut 8 strips 2½″ × width of fabric.

BACKING FABRIC: 5 yards

BATTING: 88″ × 88″

Make Precut Quilts

Block Assembly

All seam allowances are ¼".

This quilt features 12 Star blocks and 13 Nine-Patch blocks.

STAR BLOCKS

1. Select 12 print charm squares for the Star block centers; set aside.

2. Cut 48 print charm squares in half diagonally to make 96 triangles.

3. Layer a print triangle on top of a solid neutral charm square with right sides together. Place it so it's slightly askew. Stitch along the long side of the triangle, using a ¼" seam allowance. Cut off the excess solid neutral charm square.

4. Press the print fabric open.

5. Trim unit to a 5" × 5" square.

6. Layer a contrasting print triangle on top of your pieced charm square. Stitch along the long side of the triangle. Trim off the excess background charm square.

7. Press the print fabric open. Trim it back down to a 5" × 5" square to finish the star point unit. Make 48 star point units total.

8. Arrange 1 reserved print charm square, 4 star point units, and 4 assorted neutral solid charm squares, as shown. Sew together as a Nine Patch block. Each completed Star block should measure 14" × 14". Make 12 Star blocks.

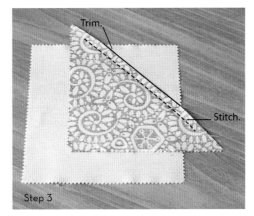

Step 3

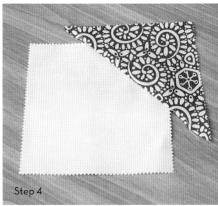

Step 4

Step 5

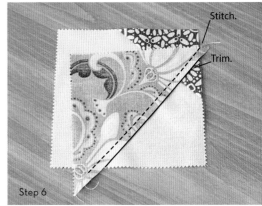

Step 6

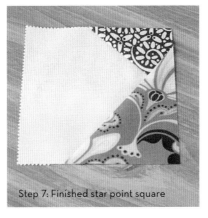

Step 7: Finished star point square

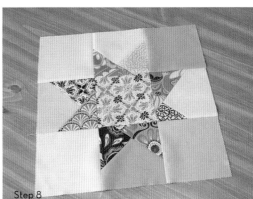

Step 8

NINE-PATCH BLOCKS

Sew 9 solid pastel charm squares to form a basic Nine-Patch block. Each completed Nine-Patch block should measure 14″ × 14″. Make 13 Nine-Patch blocks.

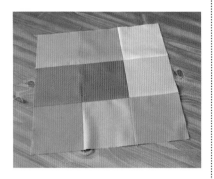

Quilt Assembly

1. Arrange all the blocks on a design wall, alternating Star blocks and Nine Patch blocks, as shown in the project photo (page 3). Sew into rows and then sew all the rows together to create the quilt top center. The quilt top center should measure 68″ × 68″.

2. Sew 4 aqua 1½″ × 45″ inner border strips together end to end to create 1 long strip. Make 2. Cut a 1½″ × 68″ strip from each strip and sew to the sides of the quilt top center. Cut a 1½″ × 70″ strip from each remaining long strip and sew to the top and bottom of the quilt top.

3. Sew 4 coral 5½″ × 45″ outer border strips together end to end to create 1 long strip. Make 2. Cut a 5½″ × 70″ strip from each long strip and sew to the sides of the quilt top. Cut a 5½″ × 80″ strip from the remaining long strips and sew to the top and bottom of the quilt top.

Quilting and Finishing

Layer, baste, quilt, and bind using your favorite methods.

Dancing Squares

Liz Aneloski

WALL/CRIB: 40½″ × 40½″
TWIN: 72½″ × 100½″
QUEEN: 88½″ × 100½″

This quilt was inspired by a wonderful line of fabric designed by Valori Wells. It would work well with almost any jelly roll. It's made using simple strip piecing and goes together quickly and easily.

Pieced by Gayle Ronconi; designed and finished by Liz Aneloski

LIZ ANELOSKI enjoys combining elements of her different passions—from using simple shapes to innovative quilting and embellishing techniques—to create new art forms. She is an editor at C&T Publishing and an author of several books and patterns. Liz lives in Northern California.

This project originally appeared in *Super Simple Jelly Roll Quilts with Alex Anderson & Liz Aneloski*, available from C&T Publishing.

Materials

Fabric	Wall/Crib	Twin	Queen
Jelly rolls (2½″ × approx. 44″ strips)	1*	3–4*	4–5*
Charm squares (5″ × 5″)	1–2 packs **	8–9 packs **	11–13 packs **
Fusible adhesive ***	1⅝ yards	6 yards	8 yards
Backing	45″ × 45″	77″ × 105″	93″ × 105″
Binding	Leftover jelly roll strips	Leftover jelly roll strips	Leftover jelly roll strips
Batting	45″ × 45″	77″ × 105″	93″ × 105″

* Based on 40 strips per jelly roll
** Based on approximately 25–30 squares per pack
*** Based on 12″ width

Cutting

Units	Wall/Crib Size of pieces; Value	Number of pieces	Twin Size of pieces; Value	Number of pieces	Queen Size of pieces; Value	Number of pieces
Horizontal background strip units	2½″ × approx. 44″; medium	20	2½″ × approx. 44″; medium	100	2½″ × approx. 44″; medium	100
Vertical background strips	2½″ × approx. 44″; dark	5	2½″ × approx. 44″; dark*	23	2½″ × approx. 44″; dark*	28
Appliqué squares (Use charm squares.)	5″ × 5″; dark	15	5″ × 5″; dark	63	5″ × 5″; dark	77
	3″ × 3″; medium	15	3″ × 3″; medium	63	3″ × 3″; medium	77
Fusible adhesive	5″ × 5″	15	5″ × 5″	63	5″ × 5″	77
	3″ × 3″	15	3″ × 3″	63	3″ × 3″	77

Sew these strips together into one long strip; then cut as directed in Step 3.

Construction

Use a ¼″ seam allowance.

1. Sew the horizontal background strips into a strip set.

NOTE: *For the twin and queen sizes:* Sew 2 strip sets, each with 50 strips.

2. Cut the strip set into 2 units 3½″ wide and 4 units 6½″ wide.

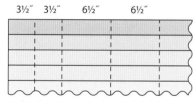

3½″ 3½″ 6½″ 6½″

Make the strip set and cut into units.

NOTES:

- *For the twin size:* Cut 2 units 3½″ wide and 8 units 6½″ wide.
- *For the queen size:* Cut 2 units 3½″ wide and 10 units 6½″ wide.

3. Measure a strip set unit from top to bottom. Trim the 5 vertical background strips to this length. Cut 9 strips for the twin; cut 11 strips for the queen.

4. Sew the units to the vertical background strips, alternating them and placing the narrower units on the outside edges. Rotate every other unit top to bottom so the fabrics are in the opposite order. Press the seam allowances toward the vertical background strips.

5. Fuse the adhesive squares to the wrong side of the corresponding-size fabric squares, following the manufacturer's instructions.

6. Fuse the 5″ × 5″ squares to the quilt top, referring to the project photo or the quilt sizing diagram for placement. Then fuse the 3″ × 3″ squares to the center of the 5″ × 5″ squares.

Wall/Crib　　　Twin　　　Queen

Quilt sizing

Finishing

1. Layer and baste the quilt.

2. Quilt as desired.

On the 5″ squares, I also machine quilted ⅛″ from the outside edges. On the 3″ squares, I machine quilted diagonally from corner to corner in both directions.

3. Bind the quilt.

I Can Sing a Rainbow Quilt

Allison Nicoll

FINISHED QUILT: 48″ × 64½″

FINISHED BLOCK: 9½″ × 8″

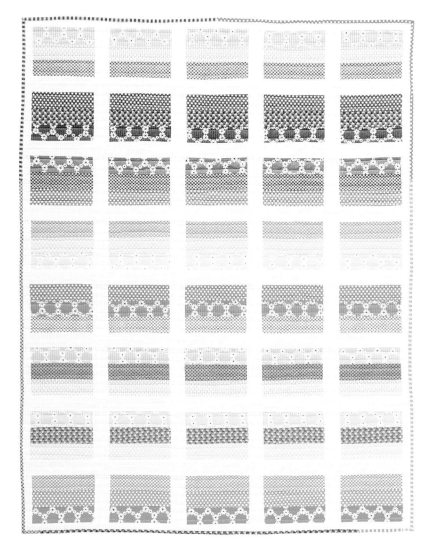

ALLISON NICOLL, known as Ally—the person behind the popular Quilting Mumma—is a respected sewing teacher. She teaches kids and young adults in her local quilt shop, and she's a Riley Blake Cutting Corners instructor. Allison lives near Sydney, Australia.

WEBSITE:
facebook.com/quiltingmumma

This project originally appeared in *Sew It!* by Allison Nicoll, available from FunStitch Studio.

Don't you just love all these bright colors? When you pick your precut roll for this quilt, look for one that has at least three strips of each color but in different patterns. If you like the quilt block but don't want the rainbow look, have fun picking out other colors.

Fabrics: Happy Tones by Michael Miller

Materials

PRINT FABRIC STRIPS: 30 strips, 2½″ wide

WHITE FABRIC: 1½ yards

BACKING: 3 yards

BATTING: 52″ × 69″

NOTE: Before You Start

- Read through all the instructions before doing any cutting or sewing.

- If you don't know how to do something or you don't remember, go back to that section in the book and find out how.

Instructions

Seam allowances are ¼″.

MAKE THE BLOCKS

1. Choose 24 strips for the blocks and 6 strips for the binding. Set aside the binding strips.

2. Place the strips for the blocks into groups of 3. You will have a total of 8 groups. Look at the quilt photo to see how the colors are grouped together. You may want to group your strips by colors or patterns. Play with them until you like the groups.

3. Stitch together each group of 3 strips into *strip sets*. Press the seam allowances all in the same direction. Trim the ends of each strip set so they are even.

4. Cut each strip set into 8″ pieces. You will have 5 pieces from each strip set.

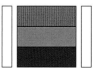

5. From the white fabric, cut 34 strips 1½″ wide across the width of the fabric. Trim off the selvages on the strips. Crosscut the strips into:

    80 strips 1½″ × 6½″

    80 strips 1½″ × 10″

6. Stitch white 1½″ × 6½″ strips to both ends of each 8″ strip set section. Press the seams *away* from the white fabric.

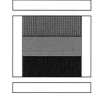
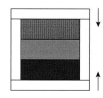

7. Stitch white 1½″ × 10″ strips to the top and bottom of each 8″ strip set section. Press the seams *away* from the white fabric.

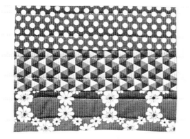
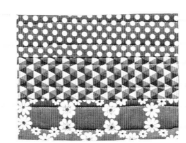
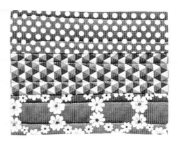

PUT TOGETHER THE QUILT

1. Look at the project photo (page 10) and the quilt assembly diagram (below) to arrange the blocks into 8 rows with 5 blocks in each row. The quilt in the photo has the blocks in color order, but you might want a different arrangement. Play with the placement until you like the way it looks.

2. Stitch the blocks into rows, nesting and pressing the seams. Press the odd-row seams to the right and the even-row seams to the left.

3. Stitch together the rows to complete the quilt top. Give the top a good pressing to make sure all the seams are flat and smooth.

4. Cut and piece the backing fabric to be 52″ × 68″.

5. Assemble your quilt sandwich, baste, and quilt. My quilt has straight-line quilting. Line up your walking foot along the seam as a guide. This is a very easy and doable way of quilting your quilts.

6. Use the 6 strips you set aside to add the binding.

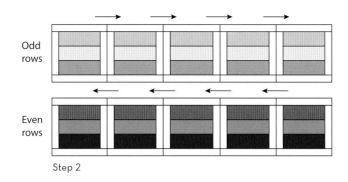

Odd rows

Even rows

Step 2

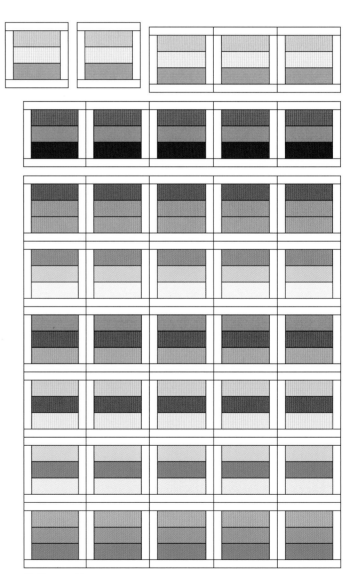

Quilt assembly

Stairways

Amanda Murphy

FINISHED QUILT: 56″ × 72″

Use a Roll-Up to create a dynamic stairway of color! Quilting a cascading design on each stair adds a special touch.

Pieced by Amanda Murphy; quilted by Deborah Norris

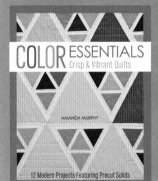

AMANDA MURPHY worked as a graphic designer and art director before she discovered quilting. She markets quilt patterns under the Amanda Murphy Designs label, and is a C&T author, a fabric designer, a Craftsy teacher, and a BERNINA quilting and longarm spokesperson. She lives in North Carolina.

WEBSITE:
amandamurphydesign.com

This project originally appeared in *Color Essentials—Crisp and Vibrant Quilts* **by Amanda Murphy, available from Stash Books.**

Materials

BLOCKS: 1 Kona Bright Roll-Up
(or 23 strips 2½" wide)

BACKGROUND: 2½ yards
Kona 1387 White

INNER BORDER: ⅓ yard
Kona 1370 Tangerine

OUTER BORDER: 1 yard
Kona 1514 Robin Egg

BINDING: ⅝ yard
Kona 1514 Robin Egg

BACKING: 4¾ yards
Kona 1265 Orange

BATTING: 64" × 80"

Cutting

WOF = width of fabric

ROLL-UPS FOR BLOCKS:

Cut 21 rectangles 2½" × 10½".

Cut 23 rectangles 2½" × 8½".

Cut 2 rectangles 2½" × 6½".

Cut 2 rectangles 2½" × 4½".

Cut 102 squares 2½" × 2½".

BACKGROUND:

1. Cut 29 strips 2½" × WOF.

2. Set 6 strips aside for the background border.

Subcut the remaining 23 strips into:

1 rectangle 2½" × 10½"

45 rectangles 2½" × 8½"

4 rectangles 2½" × 6½"

48 rectangles 2½" × 4½"

41 squares 2½" × 2½"

INNER BORDER:
Cut 6 strips 1½" × WOF.

OUTER BORDER:
Cut 7 strips 4¼" × WOF.

BINDING:
Cut 8 strips 2¼" × WOF.

Block Assembly

Use a ¼" seam allowance unless noted otherwise.

PREPARATION

1. Draw a diagonal line on the back of each background square 2½" × 2½".

2. With the diagonal line oriented as shown, place a background square 2½" × 2½" on top of each of 18 Roll-Up rectangles 2½" × 8½" and 20 Roll-Up rectangles 2½" × 10½". Sew directly on the diagonal lines. Trim the seam allowances to ¼" and press them toward the background corners.

Make 18.   Make 20.

3. With the diagonal line oriented as shown, place a background square 2½" × 2½" on top of 1 Roll-Up rectangle 2½" × 4½" and 1 Roll-Up rectangle 2½" × 6½". Sew directly on the diagonal line. Trim the seam allowances to ¼" and press them toward the background corners.

Make 1 of each.

4. Join 2 Roll-Up squares 2½" × 2½" together to make a 2-square unit. Press the seams toward the darker fabric. Repeat to make 50 units. Set 2 of these units aside. (There will be 2 squares 2½" × 2½" left over.)

5. Join 2 of the 2-square units together to make a four-patch. Repeat to make 24 four-patches.

FULL BLOCK (MAKE 17)

1. Join a background rectangle 2½″ × 4½″ to each side of a four-patch and press the seams toward the four-patch. Join background rectangles 2½″ × 8½″ to the top and bottom of this unit and press the seams toward the center. Repeat to make 22 of these units. (Set 5 aside to use for partial blocks.)

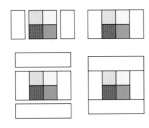

2. Join a pieced 2½″ × 8½″ unit to the bottom of a full four-patch block as shown.

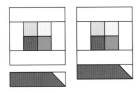

3. Join a pieced 2½″ × 10½″ unit to the left side of the full four-patch block.

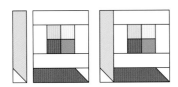

4. Repeat Steps 2 and 3 to make a total of 17 full blocks.

PARTIAL BLOCK A (MAKE 4)

Join Roll-Up rectangles 2½″ × 8½″ to the left sides of 4 units set aside in Full Block, Step 1.

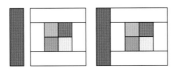

PARTIAL BLOCK B (MAKE 1)

Join a pieced rectangle 2½″ × 8½″ to the bottom of 1 unit set aside in Full Block, Step 1.

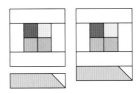

PARTIAL BLOCK C (MAKE 1)

1. Join a Roll-Up square 2½″ × 2½″ to a background rectangle 2½″ × 8½″.

2. Join this unit to a pieced 2½″ × 10½″ unit.

PARTIAL BLOCK D (MAKE 1)

1. Join a background rectangle 2½″ × 4½″ to the right side *only* of a four-patch and press the seams toward the four-patch. Join background rectangles 2½″ × 6½″ to the top and bottom of this unit and press the seams toward the center.

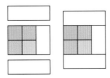

2. Join a pieced 2½″ × 6½″ unit to the bottom of the block.

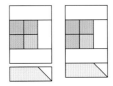

PARTIAL BLOCK E (MAKE 1)

1. Join a background rectangle 2½″ × 4½″ to the left side of a 2-square unit and press the seams toward the 2-square unit. Join background rectangles 2½″ × 4½″ to the top and bottom of this unit and press the seams toward the center.

2. Join a Roll-Up rectangle 2½″ × 4½″ unit to the bottom of the block.

3. Join a 2½″ × 10½″ unit to the left side of the block as shown.

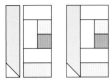

PARTIAL BLOCK F (MAKE 1)

1. Join a background rectangle 2½″ × 4½″ to the right side of a 2-square unit and press the seams toward the 2-square unit. Join background rectangles 2½″ × 4½″ to the top and bottom of this unit and press the seams toward the center.

2. Join a pieced 2½″ × 4½″ unit to the bottom of the block as shown.

PARTIAL BLOCK G (MAKE 1)

1. Join a background rectangle 2½″ × 4½″ to the left side of a four-patch and press the seam toward the four-patch. Join background rectangles 2½″ × 6½″ to the top and bottom of this unit and press the seams toward the center.

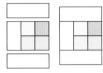

2. Join a Roll-Up rectangle 2½″ × 6½″ to the bottom of the block.

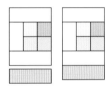

3. Join a pieced 2½″ × 10½″ unit to the left side of the block.

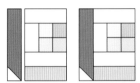

PARTIAL BLOCK H (MAKE 2)

1. Draw a diagonal line from corner to corner on the back of a Roll-Up square 2½″ × 2½″. Place the square on top of a background rectangle 2½″ × 10½″ as shown. Sew directly on the diagonal line. Trim the seams to ¼″ and press toward the corner.

Make 1.

2. Repeat with a background square 2½″ × 2½″ and a Roll-Up rectangle 2½″ × 10½″.

Make 1.

Quilt Assembly

1. Following the quilt assembly diagram, arrange the full and partial blocks to form the center of the quilt top. The bottom row will need 1 additional Roll-Up rectangle 2½″ × 8½″ sewn to the last block on the right to complete the pattern.

2. Join the blocks into rows and press the seams away from the background fabric.

3. Join the rows and press the seams upward.

My quilt top at this point measured 42½″ × 58½″. Measure your quilt in both directions through the center and adjust the border measurements that follow if needed.

4. Piece 2 rectangles 2½″ × 58½″ from the 2½″ × WOF background strips. Join to each side of the quilt top. Piece 2 rectangles 2½″ × 46½″ from the remaining 2½″ × WOF background strips and join to the top and bottom of the quilt top.

5. Piece 2 inner border rectangles 1½″ × 62½″ and join to each side of the quilt top. Piece 2 inner border rectangles 1½″ × 48½″ and join to the top and bottom of the quilt top.

6. Piece 2 outer border rectangles 4¼″ × 64½″ and join to each side of the quilt top. Piece 2 outer border rectangles 4¼″ × 56″ and join to the top and bottom of the quilt top.

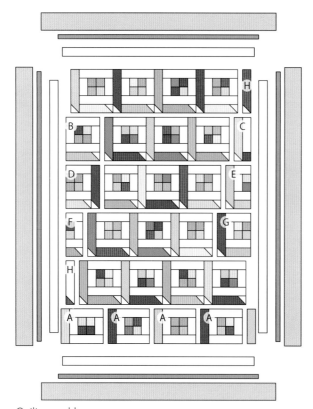

Quilt assembly

Finishing

1. Divide the backing fabric into 2 lengths. Cut 1 piece lengthwise to make 2 narrow panels. Join 1 narrow panel to each side of the wide panel. Press the seams open.

2. Layer the backing, batting, and quilt top. Baste. Quilt as desired.

3. Make the binding and bind the quilt.

Wild Webs

Mary Cowan

FINISHED QUILT: 57½" × 57½"

FINISHED BLOCK: 15½" × 15½"

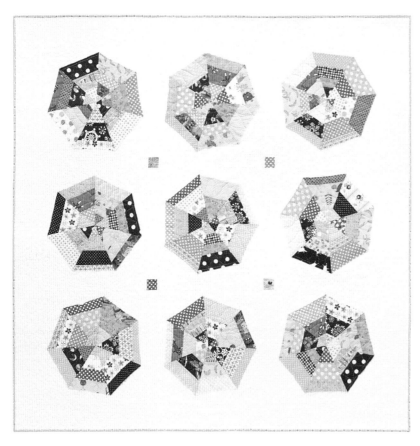

MARY COWAN is the designer behind the popular quilt pattern company Mary's Cottage Quilts. Her quilts are informed by her background in graphic design and shaped by her passion for color. Mary lives in Sandy, Utah.

WEBSITE: maryscottagequilts.com

This project originally appeared in *Colorful Stash Busters* by Mary Cowan, available from C&T Publishing.

The traditional way to make Spider Webs is to use paper piecing; instead, I used a special triangle ruler that made it so much easier! I created these Spider Webs totally from my stash of scraps. Just have fun making this—it's very easy, and the outer edges of the webs are ragged for added texture.

Designed and made by Mary Cowan; custom machine quilted by Linda Engar

Materials

BUNDLE OF PRECUT 2½"-WIDE STRIPS:*
Bright-colored fabrics (a good variety is
a must!) for webs and sashing posts

LIGHT FABRIC: 4 yards for block
backgrounds, sashing, and border

BACKING: 3¾ yards

BINDING: ½ yard

BATTING: For twin-size quilt

TRIANGLE RULER: See Tip (at right).

Option: You may use scraps instead.

tip **Triangle Ruler:** It's so easy to
make Spider Webs using the Tri-Recs
Tri Tool (from EZ Quilting) by Darlene
Zimmerman and Joy Hoffman. This is
such a cool way to make Spider Webs—
thank you, Darlene and Joy, for the
awesome ruler! This ruler measures
6½" tall and has a cut-off tip that
enables you to sew together fabric
triangles without creating a lot of bulk
in the center where all the seams
come together.

Cutting

STRIPS:

Cut 4 squares 2" × 2" for the sashing posts.

If using scraps instead of precuts, cut strips
2½", 3½", or 4" × longest measurement
of fabric.

LIGHT FABRIC:

*Before cutting, reserve a 20" × 60" piece
for the borders.*

Cut 9 squares 16" × 16" for the block
backgrounds.

Cut 12 strips 2" × 16" for the sashing.

Cut 4 strips 4½" × 60" along the *length*
of fabric for the borders.

BINDING:

Cut 7 strips 2¼" × width of fabric; sew
together using diagonal seams.

Precuts Colorway

I used a precut strip bundle (40 strips 2½" × 45") for this alternate colorway,
so it has a less scrappy look than the original quilt, which I made from my stash
fabrics, and the strips are a uniform width instead of varying widths. To vary the
width of the top and bottom strips, change the placement of the Tri Tool when
trimming to a triangle shape.

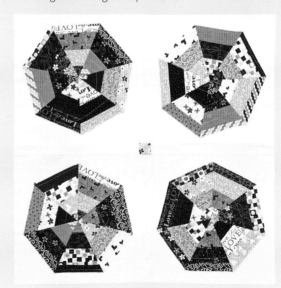

Making the Web Blocks

Make 9 blocks.

1. For the webs, sew together 4 strips of different fabrics along the long edges to make strip sets. If you are using scraps instead of precuts, you can use more or fewer than 4 strips depending on the width of your strips, but the finished width of the strip set must be at least 7½″. Press.

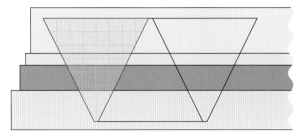

2. Center the Tri Tool top to bottom on your strip set so that you cut out a complete triangle shape. To get the greatest number of triangles out of each strip set, alternately flip the tool as shown. Cut a total of 63 triangles. You need 7 triangles to make each complete web.

Step 2

3. Pick 7 triangles that look nice together and sew them together to complete 1 web. Repeat for a total of 9 webs.

4. Cut off the dog ears that hang down past the outer edges of the webs.

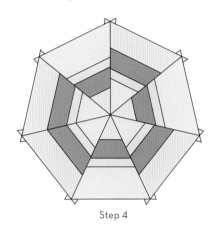

5. Center the completed web on a 16″ × 16″ background square. Pin very well and sew it to the background, starting in the middle and working out to the edges. Leave the outer edges raw so they will fray when you wash them. I sewed a funky concentric circular pattern just to hold the webs in place; the final quilting did the job of anchoring them firmly. Make sure you sew no closer than ¼″ to the outer edge of the web so it will fray nicely.

Step 4

Assembling the Quilt Top

1. Refer to the quilt assembly diagram to lay out the blocks in 3 rows; place sashing pieces between the blocks only, not at the ends of the rows. Sew together each row.

2. You will need 2 strips of sashing with posts to place between the rows. To make a sashing strip, sew together as follows: sashing piece, post, sashing piece, post, sashing piece, as shown. Repeat for the other sashing.

3. Sew together the rows and sashing. Press toward the sashing.

4. Attach the top and bottom borders and then the side borders.

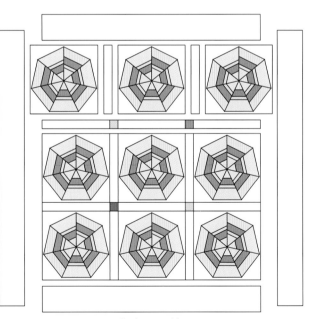

Quilt assembly

Finishing the Quilt

Note: *You will need to wash the quilt to rag the webs, but do not wash it until after finishing.*

Layer, quilt, and bind your quilt. I had this quilt custom machine quilted. I love what Linda did here with the flowers and the swirls.

RAGGING THE WEBS

Throw the finished quilt in the washer and wash in *cold* water with 1 cup of distilled white vinegar (to set the colors). Toss it in the dryer; when it is dry, your webs will have the desired "ragged" look. If some of the web edges are not frayed enough, you can squirt them with plain water from a squirt bottle, brush with a soft brush, and put the quilt back in the dryer.

Garden Days

Sherri McConnell

FINISHED QUILT: 60" × 76"

FINISHED BLOCK: 8" × 8"

SHERRI MCCONNELL, inspired by a rich family heritage of women who love sewing, began to sew at age 10. In the early 1990s, encouraged and taught by her grandmother, she began her quilting journey. Through blogging and creating, she has come to love designing and sharing her quilting. She lives in rural southern Nevada.

WEBSITE: aquiltinglife.com

This project originally appeared in *Fresh Family Traditions* by Sherri McConnell, available from C&T Publishing.

When I designed this quilt, I was trying to use one Layer Cake with little waste in order to make the biggest quilt possible. Cut carefully if using a single Layer Cake for this quilt. This quilt also makes a wonderful scrap quilt; just cut the strips and pieces from your scrap bin and have fun!

Pieced by Sherri McConnell; quilted by Natalia Bonner

Fabrics: Pam Kitty Love by Pam Vierra-McGinnis for Lakehouse Fabrics

Materials

ASSORTED PRINTS: 1 Layer Cake (42 squares 10″ × 10″) or 3⅛ yards total

WHITE SOLID: 1¾ yards

OUTER BORDER: 1⅛ yards

BINDING: ⅔ yard

BACKING: 4¾ yards

BATTING: 68″ × 84″

Cutting

ASSORTED PRINTS:
From each Layer Cake (10″ × 10″) square or assorted fabrics, cut 2 strips 1½″ × 8½″ and 2 strips 1½″ × 6½″ (42 matching sets).

From remaining Layer Cake squares or assorted fabrics, cut a total of 42 strips 2½″ × 10″ and 36 strips 1½″ × 6½″.

WHITE SOLID:
Cut 30 strips 1½″ × width of fabric; subcut into:

   12 strips 1½″ × 8½″ for blocks

   96 strips 1½″ × 6½″ for blocks

   84 strips 1½″ × 4½″ for blocks

Cut 6 strips 2″ × width of fabric for inner border.

OUTER BORDER:
Cut 7 strips 5″ × width of fabric for outer border.

BINDING:
Cut 8 strips 2½″ × width of fabric.

Block Assembly

Seam allowances are ¼″ unless otherwise noted.

1. Sew together 2 assorted print 2½″ × 10″ strips. Press toward the darker strip. Repeat to make 21 sets. Cut each strip set into 4 segments 2½″ × 4½″ for a total of 84.

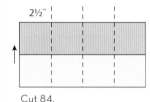

Cut 84.

2. Join 2 different segments from Step 1 to make Four-Patch blocks. Make 42.

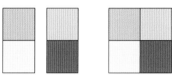

Make 42.

3. Sew the white 1½″ × 4½″ strips to the left and right sides of all the Four-Patch units from Step 2. Press toward the white strips. Sew the white 1½″ × 6½″ strips to the top and bottom of all the units. Press toward the white strips.

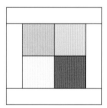

Add white strips.

4. Sew matching 1½″ × 6½″ strips to the left and right sides of the units from Step 3. Press toward the outer strips. Sew matching 1½″ × 8½″ strips to the top and bottom of the units. Press toward the outer strips. Blocks should now measure 8½″ × 8½″.

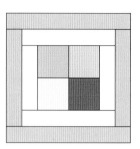

Make 42.

5. Sew together 6 different 1½″ × 6½″ print strips as shown to make a Rail Fence unit. Press the seams in one direction. Make 6.

Make 6.

6. Sew white 1½″ × 6½″ strips to the left and right sides of the units from Step 5. Press toward the white fabrics. Sew white 1½″ × 8½″ strips to the top and bottom. Press toward the white fabrics. Make 6 blocks.

Make 6.

Quilt Assembly

1. Arrange the blocks into 8 rows of 6 blocks each. Rotate every other block so that seams won't have to be aligned when sewing. Randomly place the Rail Fence–style blocks throughout the quilt top.

2. Sew the blocks in each row together. Alternate the pressing direction for each row so that the seams will nest when the rows are sewn together. Sew the rows together. Press seams in one direction.

3. Add 2″ × 64½″ inner border strips to the left and right sides of the quilt. Press toward the inner borders. Add 2″ × 51½″ inner border strips to the top and bottom of the quilt. Press toward the inner borders.

4. Add 5″ × 67½″ outer border strips to the left and right sides of the quilt. Press toward the outer borders. Add 5″ × 60½″ outer border strips to the top and bottom of the quilt. Press toward the outer borders.

5. Layer the backing, batting, and quilt top. Quilt as desired. Bind the edges.

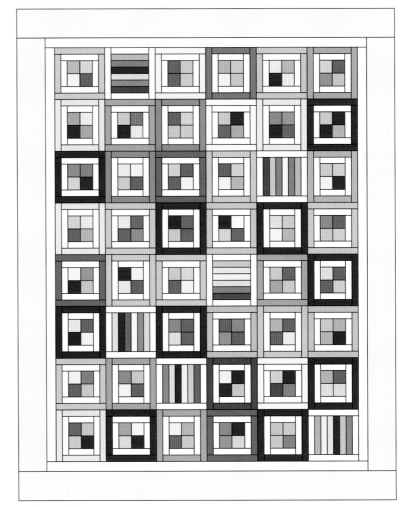

Quilt assembly

Hugs and Kisses

Cheryl Arkison

This quilt comes entirely from a sketch my daughter made. She was learning how to play tic-tac-toe, and her random scratches of X's and O's struck me for their graphic nature. Together we drew and came up with this quilt. The X's and O's are raw-edge appliquéd to the background pieces. Piece the X's precisely or in an improv style. Hand appliqué the O's for a more refined look.

CHERYL ARKISON has been sewing her entire life, which has developed into her talents as a quilter, pattern designer, book author, magazine writer, teacher, and blogger (on Dining Room Empire) about quilting and crafts, as well as creativity, food, and family. Cheryl lives in Alberta, Canada.

WEBSITE: cherylarkison.com

This project originally appeared in *A Month of Sundays—Family, Friends, Food & Quilts* by Cheryl Arkison, available from Stash Books.

Materials

Amounts are based on a fabric width of 42".

QUILT TOP: 3 Layer Cakes or 35 fat quarters (for maximum variety)

BATTING: 94" × 67"

BACKING: 5½ yards

BINDING: ¾ yard

FREEZER PAPER (OPTIONAL)

FABRIC GLUE OR LIGHTWEIGHT FUSIBLE WEB (OPTIONAL)

Cutting

QUILT TOP:
Cut 2 squares 9½" × 9½" from each fat quarter for a total of 70 squares.

X'S AND O'S:
Draw a template for the O's using a compass, 2 bowls/plates, or freehand to create an O shape no longer or wider than 8". The width of the "lines" that make up the O should be about 1½"– 2". Cut out your template.

Draw a template for the X's using a ruler or by eye. The X should be no longer or wider than 8". The width of the "lines" that make up the X should be about 1½"– 2". Cut out your template.

Cut 18 O's and 24 X's from a variety of fabrics and appliqué, using fusible web and the manufacturer's directions.

BINDING:
Cut as needed for your preferred method of binding.

Some Assembly Required

Seam allowances are ¼".

1. Pair up the X's and O's with background squares. Evaluate the value to make sure there is contrast between the appliqué and the background.

2. Appliqué the X's and O's to the background blocks.

3. Arrange the blocks into 7 rows of 10 blocks each. You can follow the quilt top assembly diagram or arrange the blocks in a way that works for you. (For that matter, you can also make more or less appliqués to suit your design preference.)

4. Assemble the quilt top using chain piecing. If you are pressing the seams to one side, be sure to alternate the direction so the seams nest when you sew together the rows.

5. Sew the rows together and press the seams open or in one direction.

6. Assemble the quilt back to measure 94" × 67".

7. Layer the backing, batting, and quilt top. Baste with your preferred method.

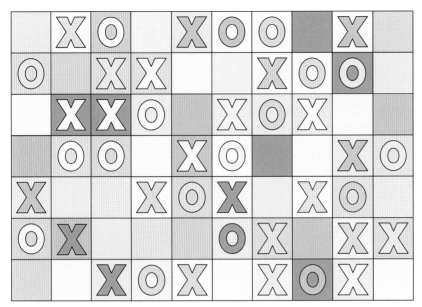

Quilt top assembly

Ready, Set, Quilt!

You have choices when it comes to quilting this quilt. You can outline your X's and O's by repeating the appliqué stitching and then stitch a background design. Or you can stitch an allover design that tacks down the raw-edge appliqué. This quilt will look better the more it is used and washed, so don't fuss too much about the quilting—those raw edges will become nice and soft over time.

Finishing

Trim the excess batting and backing, square up the quilt, and attach the binding.

Turn Up the Volume

Pick your favorite color combination to give a whole pile of hugs and kisses to someone you love. A single background color with bold choices for the X's and O's is a surefire way to declare your love from the rooftops for all to hear.

Playground

Camille Roskelley

FINISHED QUILT: 60″ × 72″

FINISHED BLOCK: 12″ × 12″

CAMILLE ROSKELLEY Growing up in a home brimming with creativity and quilts, Camille became a talented quilter and designer. She's now a fabric designer for Moda, a book author, a Craftsy quilting teacher, and a quilt pattern designer for her own company, Thimble Blossoms. Camille lives in Las Vegas, Nevada.

WEBSITE: camilleroskelley.com

This project originally appeared in *Simply Retro with Camille Roskelley*, available from Stash Books.

We've spent a lot of time at the playground over the last eight years. When my oldest boys were young, we were there just about every day. They loved it there, and I loved how much they loved it! Looking at this quilt in their bedroom reminds me of that playground, where we spent our days when my big boys were little guys—and, well, that I just don't want to forget.

Pieced by Camille Roskelley; quilted by Tami Bradley

Fabric: Reunion by Sweetwater for Moda

Materials

Yardages are based on 42″-wide fabric.

BLOCKS:

    36 Layer Cake squares 10″ × 10″

    2¼ yards of neutral fabric

BACKING: 3⅞ yards

BINDING: ⅝ yard

BATTING: 64″ × 76″

Cutting

LAYER CAKE SQUARES:

Cut 12 squares into smaller squares 4⅞″ × 4⅞″ (4 smaller squares from each Layer Cake square, for a total of 48) for the half-square triangles (HSTs).*

Cut 24 squares into 4 smaller squares 4½″ × 4½″ (4 smaller squares from each Layer Cake square, for a total of 96) for the blocks.

NEUTRAL FABRIC:

Cut 6 strips 4⅞″ × WOF;** subcut squares 4⅞″ × 4⅞″ (8 per strip, for a total of 48) for the HSTs.

Cut 10 strips 4½″ × WOF.

    From 7 strips, subcut pieces 4½″ × 12½″ (3 per strip, for a total of 21) for the sashing.

    From 3 strips, subcut squares 4½″ × 4½″ (9 per strip, for a total of 21) for the blocks.

BINDING:

Cut 7 strips 2½″ × WOF.

Each Layer Cake square paired with a neutral square will yield 8 HSTs.
** WOF = width of fabric

Block Assembly

This quilt is made up of 21 full blocks and 6 partial blocks. First make 96 HSTs using the 48 squares 4⅞″ × 4⅞″ cut from the Layer Cakes and the white squares 4⅞″ × 4⅞″.

To make half-square triangles (HSTs), place 1 square on top of the other with right sides together (**a**). On the back of the lighter square, draw a pencil line from one corner to the opposite corner (**b**). Sew ¼″ from the line on each side (**c**). Cut on the line to make 2 HSTs (**d**). Press toward the darker of the 2 fabrics.

a   b   c   d

FULL BLOCKS

For each of the full blocks, you will need 4 matching HSTs, 4 matching Layer Cake squares 4½″ × 4½″, and 1 white square 4½″ × 4½″.

1. Refer to the full-block assembly diagram to sew together the pieces into 3 rows of 3. Press. Sew together the rows to make 1 full block. Press.

2. Repeat to make a total of 21 blocks.

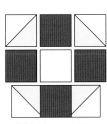

Full-block assembly

PARTIAL BLOCKS

For each of the partial blocks, you will need 2 matching HSTs and 1 Layer Cake square 4½″ × 4½″. Sew together the pieces as shown in the partial-block assembly diagram. Press. Repeat to make a total of 6 partial blocks.

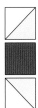

Partial-block assembly

Quilt Assembly

1. Sew 3 rows A, alternating 4 full blocks and 3 neutral strips 4½″ × 12½″. Press.

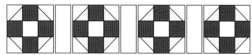

Row A assembly

2. Sew 3 rows B, alternating 3 full blocks and 4 neutral strips 4½″ × 12½″. Sew 1 partial block on each end. Press.

Row B assembly

3. Sew together the 6 rows as shown in the quilt assembly diagram. Press.

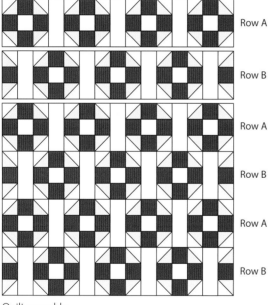

Quilt assembly

Finishing

1. Cut the backing fabric into 2 equal lengths (roughly 64″), and sew them together for the backing.

2. Layer the quilt top, batting, and backing, and pin baste to make a quilt sandwich. Machine or hand quilt as desired. Bind your quilt.

Century Farm

Sherri McConnell

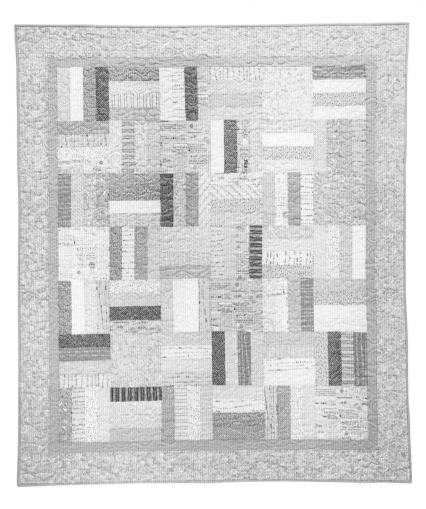

FINISHED QUILT: 59″ × 67″

FINISHED BLOCK: 8″ × 8″

SHERRI MCCONNELL, inspired by a rich family heritage of women who love sewing, began to sew at age 10. In the early 1990s, encouraged and taught by her grandmother, she began her quilting journey. Through blogging and creating, she has come to love designing and sharing her quilting. She lives in rural southern Nevada.

WEBSITE: aquiltinglife.com

This project originally appeared in *Fresh Family Traditions* by Sherri McConnell, available from C&T Publishing.

In 1985 my grandmother and her sisters were awarded the Century Farm designation for their 80 acres of Iowa farmland originally purchased by their paternal great-grandparents. This quilt is a tribute to that farm heritage as well as my grandmother's love of the Rail Fence block.

Pieced by Sherri McConnell; quilted by Gail Begay

Fabrics: Notebook by Sweetwater for Moda and Moda Bella Solids in Gray

Materials

ASSORTED PRINTS: 1 Layer Cake
(42 squares 10″ × 10″) or 3 yards total

INNER BORDER: 1/3 yard

OUTER BORDER: 1⅛ yards

BACKING: 4 yards

BINDING: 5/8 yard

BATTING: 67″ × 75″

Cutting

ASSORTED PRINTS:

From each of 35 Layer Cake squares,
cut 4 strips 2½″ × 10″ (140 total).

From each of 7 Layer Cake squares,
cut 1 square 8½″ × 8½″ (7 total).

INNER BORDER:

Cut 6 strips 1½″ × width of fabric.

OUTER BORDER:

Cut 7 strips 5″ × width of fabric.

BINDING:

Cut 7 strips 2½″ × width of fabric.

Block Assembly

Seam allowances are ¼″ unless otherwise noted.

1. Arrange the 2½″ × 10″ strips in 35 groups of 4 strips each.
Sew each set together, pressing the seams in one direction.

Make 35.

2. Trim each block to measure 8½″ × 8½″.

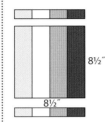

Trim.

Quilt Assembly

1. Arrange the pieced blocks and 8½" × 8½" squares in 7 rows of 6 blocks each.

2. Sew the blocks in each row together. Alternate the pressing direction for each row so that the seams will nest when the rows are sewn together. Sew the rows together. Press toward the bottom of the quilt.

3. Piece the 1½"-wide inner border strips for length; then cut into 2 strips 1½" × 56½" for left and right sides and sew to the sides of the quilt. Press toward the inner border. Cut 2 strips 1½" × 50½" for the top and bottom inner borders. Sew to the quilt and press toward the inner border strips.

4. Piece the 5"-wide outer border strips together for length; then cut into 2 strips 5" × 58½" for left and right outer borders. Sew to the sides of the quilt and press toward the outer border. Cut 2 strips 5" × 59½" for the top and bottom borders. Sew to the quilt and press toward the outer border strips.

5. Layer the backing, batting, and quilt top. Quilt as desired. Bind the edges.

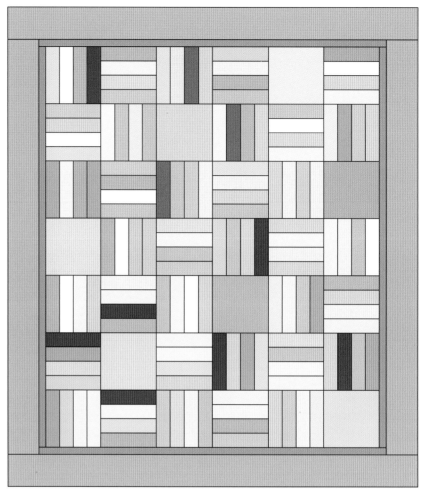

Quilt assembly

Master Suite

Sweetwater

FINISHED QUILT: 80½″ × 93½″

FINISHED BLOCK: 9″ × 9″

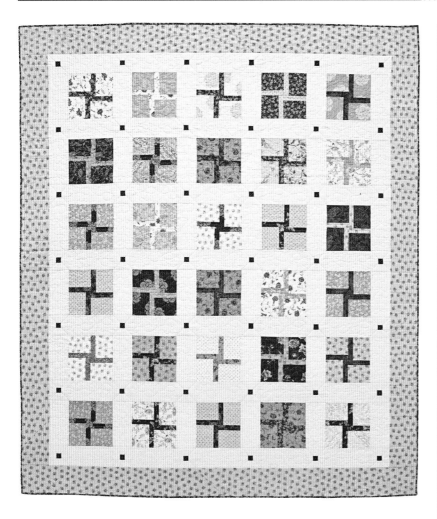

SWEETWATER was founded in 2001 by Karla Eisenach and her two daughters, Lisa Burnett and Susan Kendrick. Located in Colorado, Sweetwater's simple yet sophisticated aesthetic infuses their many product lines, including fabric and quilt patterns for Moda.

WEBSITE: thesweetwaterco.com

This project originally appeared in *Sweetwater's Simple Home* by Karla Eisenach, Lisa Burnett, and Susan Kendrick, available from Stash Books.

Although this queen-size quilt isn't one you will complete in an afternoon, it truly is simple to make, and it's so satisfying to use and admire when it's all finished.

Designed and made by Sweetwater; machine quilted by Brian Clements

Materials

BLOCKS:

    30 different prints, each cut 10″ × 10″, or 10″ × 10″ precut pack

    30 different prints, each cut 1½″ × width of fabric, or 1½″-wide strip bundle

SASHING CORNERSTONES:

    ⅛ yard solid red fabric

    1 yard solid cream fabric

SASHING: 2½ yards solid cream fabric

BORDERS: 1¾ yards

BINDING: ¾ yard

BACKING: 88″ × 101″

BATTING: 88″ × 101″

Instructions

A ¼″ seam allowance is included.

BLOCKS

1. Cut 4 pieces 5″ × 4″ from a 10″ × 10″ print square.

2. Cut 4 pieces 5″ × 1½″ from a print strip.

3. With right sides together, sew a 5″ × 1½″ piece to each 5″ × 4″ piece along the 5″ side. Press the seams to one side.

Make 4.

4. Sew the 4 pieces together as shown to make 1 block 9½″ × 9½″ unfinished.

5. Repeat Steps 1–4 to make a total of 30 blocks.

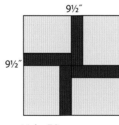

Make 30.

SASHING CORNERSTONES

1. Cut 2 strips 1½″ × the width of the fabric from the red sashing cornerstone fabric. Subcut the strips into 42 squares 1½″ × 1½″.

2. Cut 4 strips 2″ × the width of the fabric from the cream sashing cornerstone fabric. Subcut the strips into 84 pieces 2″ × 1½″.

3. Sew 2 pieces of cream fabric to opposite sides of a red square.

4. Cut 11 strips 2″ × the width of the fabric from the cream fabric. Subcut the strips into 84 pieces 2″ × 4½″.

5. Sew the 2″ × 4½″ pieces of cream fabric to the sides of the red square unit as shown.

6. Repeat Steps 1–5 to make a total of 42 sashing cornerstones 4½″ × 4½″ (unfinished).

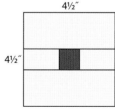

Make 42.

SASHING

1. Cut 18 strips 4½" × the width of the fabric from the sashing fabric. Subcut the 18 strips into 71 pieces 4½" × 9½".

2. Sew sashing pieces between the blocks and at both ends to make a row with 5 blocks. Press toward the sashing.

3. Repeat Step 2 with the remaining blocks to make a total of 6 rows.

4. Sew sashing corners between the sashing pieces and at both ends to make a strip with 6 sashing corners. Press toward the sashing.

5. Repeat Step 4 with the remaining sashing corners to make a total of 7 strips.

6. Referring to the quilt assembly diagram, sew the strips in between the rows and at both ends, pressing toward the sashing rows as you go along.

BORDERS

1. Cut 9 strips 6" × the width of the fabric.

2. Sew the border strips to the sides, top, and bottom of the quilt.

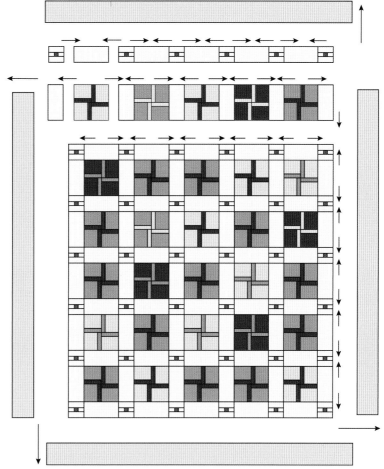

Quilt assembly

FINISHING

For the binding, cut 10 strips 2¼" × the width of the fabric; sew together using diagonal seams to make 1 long strip.

Layer, quilt, and bind the quilt. Quilt your quilt top as desired. Our quilt features an allover leaf and vine design.

Make Precut Quilts